1 9 8 9

IN THE NORTH

IN THE NORTH

POETRY BY

NINA BOGIN

GRAYWOLF PRESS
SAINT PAUL

The author wishes to express her deepest gratitude to Magda Bogin
for her encouragement, her generosity, and her fine critical eye.

Acknowledgments
Some of the poems in this collection first appeared
in the following magazines:
Agenda: "Prophecy," "Wild Heather";
American Poetry Review: "Bologna, November";
California Quarterly: "St. Valentin," "In Bavaria";
The Iowa Review: "It Was Not a Star," "The Kettle Hums,"
    "Like a Wound," "Once Again the Moon," "A Sky of Dark
    Furrows";
Ironwood: "The Garden," "Under";
The Kenyon Review: "Initiation," "Wild Plums in August,"
    "Through Marshland";
Stand: "The Caught Fish Speaks," "In the North," "Under."

Publication of this volume is made possible by generous donations
Graywolf Press receives from corporations, foundations and
individuals, including the Minnesota State Arts Board and the
National Endowment for the Arts. Graywolf is a member organization
of United Arts, Saint Paul, and a recipient of a McKnight Award.

Library of Congress Cataloguing-in-Publication Data
Bogin, Nina.
    In the North : poetry / by Nina Bogin.
        p.   cm.
    ISBN 1-55597-121-0 : $14.00
    I. Title.
PS3552.0439516   1989
811'.54--dc 20   89-33226

First Printing, 1989
9 8 7 6 5 4 3 2

Published by Graywolf Press,
Post Office Box 75006
Saint Paul, Minnesota 55175

For Ruth Bogin, my mother,

and in memory of George Bogin, my father,

the first Bogin poet.

TABLE OF CONTENTS

PROPHECY

IN THE NORTH

I N S I D E   T H E   S T I R

"Sadness was the form, happiness the content."

—MILAN KUNDERA,
The Unbearable Lightness of Being

PROPHECY

INITIATION

I.

At that time, a bottle of dark wine
was a life, or the hope
of a single evening —
I thought it would be like that.
There were details, onions in a bowl,
quarters of lemon rocking
on the dark-grained table,
a linen cloth folded and folded
into an immaculate square.
Men's faces ringed the table,
desiring what was white.
I wanted the future, its wine embrace.

II.

At the crossroads, hens scratched circles
into the white dust. There was a shop
where I bought coffee and eggs, coarse-grained
chocolate almost too sweet to eat.
When I walked up the road, the string sack
heavy on my arm, I thought
that my legs could take me anywhere,
into any country, any life.
The air, dazzling as sand, grew dense
with light: bougainvillea spilled
over the salmon walls, the road
veered into the ravine. The world
could be those colors, the mangoes,
the melons, the avocado evenings
releasing their circles of moon.
I climbed the pink stairs, entered
the house as calm and ephemeral
as my own certainty:
this is my house, my key,
my hand with its new lines.
I am as old as I will ever be.

BOLOGNA, NOVEMBER

On the dark day
after the Day of the Dead,
fog belled over the small
churches. Under blackened domes,
the broken light of tapers
searched out the forgotten
sacrifices, the defiant beasts
in their worn colors, the stark
angels and the dolorous
faces of the long blessed,
blazing, blazing.

It is my sister and I in Bologna
in the first breath
of winter, holding our hands
to the candle's mouth.
How we would like to believe
that what preceded us
was magnificent in suffering!
O flame and sorrow,
let us believe
that what we become
is no more than our lives
gathering their colors
into that incandescence. . .

ST. VALENTIN

Ice clamps down over Paris
like a bell. They say

the river's rising, they say
the wind drowns in the din.

This tight-lipped night won't let
any saints in,

it means to break the thin
glass threads. Once

the white walls shook
till they bled. Now

the days are edged in blue,
I don't count them, I make them do.

I know
this cold night

that rocks us in its swell.
It rings clear, it tells

of the bitter morning,
the scarred sun

warning, warning.

PROPHECY

Little red flower, push
your way into his hand,

ply through his fingers,
take root in his palm.

Red-mouth, he will bow over you
with such tenderness,

will hold you like a bird,
an early hour,

you will fill like a bell,
his kindness will brim

into you like dew.

IN BAVARIA

Blue and white jugs sit
on your shelf. They are pleased
and thick, stone-lipped.
They want honey

or cream, things
you don't like.
Sweets frighten you, they are
too much to want.

You are sharp
and thin, a tinny string.
Your husband's a soft shoe,
he counts on you.

Only the morning cheers you,
it's so pure.
There are your neighbors, your cars.
Even the streets are new.

Munich suits you, it's clean and flat.
You offer us bikes, you give us a map.
You'll drive us anywhere.

The shops wink at us, it's all a big joke.
Everyone smiles, everyone is kind.
And their faces

open to us, blindly, like smooth
white pitchers waiting
to be filled.

THE ABSENT

This they did not speak of,
or called by another name —

sweet-pea was the flower
they didn't find.

Snakes hid under the rushes.
Berries grew along the brook.

Each step they took was on firm ground.
Looking back, they saw

the farthest hill darkened by a cloud.
Even the earth knew

no such word as
"forgetting-of-the-unbegotten."

HORSES IN A FIELD IN BELGIUM

The horses move together
under the steel grimace of rain.

Flank to flank, heads meeting
in the inner circle,

they wait like the dark spokes
of a wheel at rest.

SELF-PORTRAIT

for Paula Modersohn-Becker (1876–1907)

Daughter, this is the cruel gift,
these eyes that know you.
The deep blues and yellows,
the frank mouth –
I looked hard into myself
and saw the woman I would be for you.
Let the colors speak!
To live was to paint.

It was this woman, myself,
I learned to know best.
I could no longer trick myself,
or shy from solitude:
even disappointment became a strength in me.
I worked, worked
towards this clarity –
knowing my thirty years,
and each painting the first.

Then you, child, white anemone, bloomed.
How I loved you, and did not fear you –
you were my life, flying out from my hands
like feathers or seeds,
each with its task
and its blackness . . .

Then I drifted from you and all others,
leaving behind me
this wake of colors,
a woman leaning from a painting,
offering a life.

WORDS

Today the sky is a mud-yellow,
clouds like dirty laundry,
and I was beginning to get so tired
of the tree trunk, the bird,
the snow-covered roof.
I wanted the sky to crack open
and something terrible and sulfurous
to leak out, billowing over these foothills
and wrapping us all in some new
vocabulary, something we'd never heard of,
that we couldn't articulate.
Or maybe it has already happened,
and I'm inside it,
bound up like a mummy in invisible
yellow gauze, my mouth open
against the mesh, the words
stuck and harsh in the choked air,
new and unintelligible
like acid, like rust . . .

IN THESE FIELDS

Thoughts turn on their axle.
Roads move out under rain.
Memories offer themselves

like destinations or burdens.
They follow me from the houses,
from the armoires, but they are colorless,

and their circle of faces
does not move me, not now, when the fields
are dense beneath bundled clouds.

A long way behind me
a girl in a red scarf
walks the wet fields.

She leans forward in thought,
her face pale and luminous,
not needing me,

and it is precisely she
I wanted to remember.

IN THE NORTH

WILD PLUMS IN AUGUST

As long shadows
slip into the valley,
we grow thirsty.
Sun sits on our shoulders
like a hawk
whose eyes seize
the stark shift of season.
In the dark
of pines, it could be
night.
Your hand
on my neck drinks
the cold.

Sheep
are tearing the high grass
as we walk back.
In the field, among
the other flowers,
autumn crocus opens
in its hour.
And the orchard
is scattered
with hard-eyed plums.
You bend
to gather some.
They are blue

and warm
in our palms.
As we eat
them, love
fills us
with its calm.

ALL SOULS

The shorn fields
expose their ribs,

and the dead
bear the last

sheaves gathered
at their breast.

Now the living
return to their

hearths, and the moon
in a ring of ice

appears in each windowpane,
wavering, already

forgotten, like all things
too small or too great –

what is this longing, they whisper,
there is no reason –

the eiderdowns are folded
back, and the married

and the celibate
enter a white sleep

already drifted through
with dreams,

and the moon in its
plenitude pardons them.

WILD HEATHER

Stone wanted a martyr,
who wanted a terrain —
this is the field

strewn with rock, with thorn.
Nothing grows here
but what is cruel —

spiked holly, thistles outsized
and enraged. The earth
gives itself up to pain.

Now wild heather quickens
to the wound, blue-red
and amazed

at so much incompetence.
It would teach us
tenacity —

the relentless dark blooms
sinking their roots
into the stone —

this cannot be undone.

EVERY STREET IS A RIVER

Every street is a river
that might sweep away
girls in blue cotton dresses
dreaming of wind.
The screened windows
with their odor of grass
give them nights
of dense promise —
moons rise
on their breath,
leaves unclothe them.
Even the small blue flowers
are embraces

as tonight the snow
is blue under twilight
and the river smokes
in the copses.
The familiar stars
comb through strands of cloud,
and it has all happened,
the wind in the skirts,
the mist streaming through streets
and the moon
raising its horn over the hours,
assembling all we have been
or dreamed of, girls in blue dresses,
blue flowers.

IN THE NORTH

It is natural
there should be this waste —

the apples lost
to rain, the slow

renunciation
of the branches.

Yet the absence
of a single lemon tree

surprises me, although
no such trees are found here.

It is not always possible
to be vigilant.

And love, in its
negligence,

is laid bare again,

first the recognition,
then the dark
stirring as of leaves.

NEW MOON

The owl
that raked the night with its
scream, blackened
my chest with fear —
what animal
stiffened in the road, its breath
withheld, like the tree
whose roots clutch the air
over the precipice,
it will fall,
all will fall,
the stones
with their hiss
leaving the unspoken
vowel,
the night, gouged out.

I did not drown.
I did not call things by their name.
I had no siblings.
I was not a martyr.

I lived.

Now the last blood
washes through me –
my memories.

What I miss
is the silence.

LOST ONE

The days have done with you.
On a far hill the black
firs lose themselves in fog.

The morning is torn,
the sky flung out.
Rain drifts down

like something remembered
or once living –
how pure this absence is,

flaming up gold,
these wings, these ashes,
anything the imagination

cannot hold onto.
The little brooks carry you away,
as if you were substantial,

as if there were a river
that could contain you.

VERNAL

The dark weeds, the drenched
odor of lilacs.
It is the child come back
to my arms, his skin
humid, smelling of leaves.
He has been left outside
and the flowers
have grown up around him,
white lilies, white narcissus.
How wise he is, his face
floating over us
like the vernal moon,
his hands so precise —
these are petals,
these are fruit.
We walk through the grass
at twilight, the blue thistles
flaming, the fields
falling off into night.
The still air rises,
the sky holds us
in the bowl of its hands,
the living and the dead,
a fistful of violets
or early stars
for this lost spring.

UNDER

Something's been plucked out.
The tiniest of cries
goes unheard.

Little fist, little foot,
darkness loves you.
A fissure opens

in the body of black.
Thick roots twist you down
to the great gap stirring its silences.

This is where the flat rocks dredge their shadows,
where the thin mineral air occurs.
I will rest here, a little while.

I will love this night.
The musty onions come to fruit.
I eat bits of earth,

I knit little socks and hats.
I am the mother
of the hidden ones,

the seed-eaters, the blind diggers.
Mud warms them.
Rain is their milk.

Wingless and voiceless, they grub
among the wet stumps and tubers.
Their dumb lives hum

with the hope of the ordinary.
The belly of the underworld fattens.
I'll beget another.

THROUGH MARSHLAND

In this field are beginnings, green hearts
that bear violets, shadow-loving sorrel.

Their green is sleek with the memory of ice;
even now they are separate as flowers.

I too am a sort of leaf; I have two hearts,
and my body is the globe

where a new child winters. Snow-swollen
streams run underfoot. My heels sink

in last year's grass. So much has grown over.
From the footbridge, a year ago, we gave

the ashes of our firstborn to the water.
When I walk here, the twined wet

branches of the beech trees comfort me
with their lines of darkness.

It is a slow learning. I am only myself,
what I know, what I love.

Some days, I am immense with strength,
a tree listening

to the murmur of its tap root.
A stillness enters me.

Or it is my feet going where they want to go,
and I follow, through marshland,

over the matted stalks.
And suddenly there is the gold

globe of the marshflower,
its five distinct petals rising

like suns out of the water.

THE GARDEN

Late green day.
Here's happiness with its edge of frost.
Winter's in.

The sky thins out.
The world tightens, like a walnut.
I can count most things.

The plum trees are taut on their hill,
the mornings bitten off, like a twig.
The earth will give and give.

INSIDE
THE STIR

BEACH

That clarity – a small girl in a sailor dress,
the wind slapping against her legs,
and an event, her life, about to occur,
the sand-white world unfolding at her feet,
the ocean bright as mica and approving
as she stands in the dune's soft palm
and knows, in that moment, who she is.

ECLIPSE

I had dressed for maturity. Already
the bruised violets had been wrung out of the earth,
the snows dissolved into murmurings. I lifted up
my robes, heavy with constellations. The world
stilled, in fear; I was concerned
with my profile, the blue shadows of my thighs. Never
had I been so ready, so cold with burning. Then the vision
of my intended seized me with dazzlement;
I caught myself passing my hand across
my face, as if in hesitation. Then
I bore down on him;
a blackness like heat seared into me.

THE STONE

"Tola erected this stone for his son Harold, brother of Ingvar. They undertook many voyages – very far – in search of gold, and in the East they did the eagles' bidding – they died in the South – in Serkland."

– inscription on a stone outside Gripsholm Castle, Sweden

Listen: the sea rolled back leaving
its stripped rocks. My sons
stood there, fair-haired, their swords
gleaming across their chests.
Then the long boats bore them away.
The clouds are torn and hurried, the far blue
a dream I followed all my days.
I too was a warrior. Now my arms
are grey with sinews, like the eagle
too weary for the hunt, his slate-smooth
head bowed low upon his breast.
We are sadly plumaged.

But the gods
have given us stone, harsh
and beautiful. So I will carve
pain and love, that are inseparable,
into what is immutable. May it bear my truth
for all time: I am a broken man.

SUMMER

Cows softly tread the shadows: it is morning.

All day the field will follow them,
greening under their hooves.

THE SLEEPERS

The torturers
sleep or do not sleep,
dreaming of brightly lit
corridors that keep them awake.
The houses are eyes squeezed shut.
Flowers waste their perfumes overnight.

The others, in sleep, climb interminable
flights of stairs toward the window
which opens onto the roof.
It is dawn and the tiles gleam with dew.
Clothes on lines fan the air like wings.

There, in the violet bay, glides the boat
that will take them to a neighboring country.
There is the suitcase with the false papers
and few belongings, the rope ladder,
the gloves, the helping friends.
Hands ease them down the swaying rungs,
guide them on hushed tires through the city
quiet as a beating heart.
The quay smells of promise and salt.
Now the anchor lifts, the sails
fill with shadow.
The prow heads north or south or east or west.
And the boat rocks, rocking
the sleepers into the night
sealed up like a letter, unsent.

THE BREAKING OF CAMP
OF THE VISIGOTH KING

Day of metal, the wind clanging.
In a circle of trees, they were fitting the crown
on the young king's head. Gold, bits of color —
the horses stamped

in the uneasy shadows. Soon the marshes
would be flats of ice, wolves steal close
to the homesteads. All along the hillside
the brass of leaves

whispered of the dead: over and over again
clouds scattering, light breaking
over swords and jewels. From one end of forest

to another, the dark of history,
all it forgets. Stir of bronze and leather.
The last fire quenched.

IT WAS NOT A STAR

It was not a star unloosened from its hold, not
the night turned inside out
by a needle catching up its threads,

it was the hours
whispering about imperfection, the words
we simply will not admit,

those graceless truths that prick us
under the skin — call them
the smaller cruelties,

so easy, like jewels —
and we have the gall
to aspire to purity,

that image of glass
that sits there
placidly stitching layettes,

blonde and able to smile
albeit abstractedly at the children
pulling at her skirts —

here is a kiss for her lover,
behind the ear, here is a
biscuit for the cat —

but the real
skirt is a lapful
of pins, that draw

real blood and hurt even
as the least intelligible murmur
slips under the skin

with its flicker of inevitability,
that truth recognized long ago
beyond any sky unthreading

its constellations, beyond any beauty
we would prefer to see.

THE KETTLE HUMS

The kettle hums on its blue ring. Steam
rubs the windowpanes, and everything

has become small again, even
the hours, whose creaking as of floorboards

or hidden mice is familiar, really, one of the kinder
evils, though it can, at three a.m., wake you

into terror – my life, my loved ones –
but this is what you must not

think of, this is what the friendly kettle
would protect you from as its vapor

rises so bravely
from the circle of flame.

LIKE A WOUND

Like a wound, it stitched itself
back into place. But it was not a wound,

it was the womb
taking leave of the child, the one it

loved too much, for whom it bled
uselessly, giving back all its animal

blues and mauves, its knots of nerves,
as if to say: I have done what I could,

I am not to blame. And blamelessly
closed into itself and healed. But we

had no such faith. Being simple,
we grieved that absence

and grieve it still, though it has
no name, though it sleeps

content and solitary
in its other night, having gone

back to its smallest particle
of being that exists

blackly and incomprehensibly
as a thought.

ONCE AGAIN THE MOON

Once again the moon
edges through the trees, solitary
and single-minded, staking
out its shadows — this is what

it is meant to do, and the shadows
go on trying to loosen themselves
from fixed things —
houses and trees that hold down

the darkness, that carry the moon
high overhead like a banner:
"We exist, given the presence
of our familiars."

I am like them, never far
from what I know, that I name
child, dwelling, husband, street,
as if it were impossible

to advance through the original night,
empty-handed, wordless, everything
as yet untouched by my choosing:
the house gathered around its lights,

the car locked into silence, the roads
slipping through the darkness
on their way out of the world.

A SKY OF DARK FURROWS

A sky of dark furrows. The fields flatten themselves,
prepared for anything: the wind's blade, its

neglect. On this hill I have learned so well
to wait that now I must unlearn it: nothing waits,

nothing is so empty that it does not fill
by chance or purpose and so filling become

itself; that is called choice.
And the hand, with its fixed signature,

must continue the task. Old harrow,
worrying its groove. It takes this much force

to move it through the patient field. This much
force to lift the restless hand.

M I L K

All that's astray
comes to rest,
white feathers

settling into morning.
Sleep falls away
like folds of clean linen,

and the body wakes
to a child so new
that all that surrounds her

lightens, rising like breath
around her breath.
Her claim

on the blue drift of air —
milk is forthcoming, will quiet
the steel-sharp clouds

that hug the eastern edge —
the world moves so slowly
tugging its white cords after it —

while morning
takes us under its wings,
lets her drink.

KNOWLEDGE

Summer's drowse, its sulfurous
clouds. We drift
through green, one year older,

though our knowledge is endless.
The moments sift
over us like pollen; flowers

nod in their dream. But it is real,
the child in her red dress,
her hand in my hand as her whole

taut body reaches out into a tangle
of clover as vast
and chaotic as anything she will have to learn.

THIS IS THE CITY EVENING

in memory of Marta Traba

This is the city evening, quietly exhaling
its damp; a light rain shutters the streets

into intimacy. Somewhere in this city
there is the fragrance of fruit, of cool glasses

on a glass table. And the muted voices
of the three women seated there in the natural

calm of meeting: they must be attentive
to one another, there is so much unknown,

ungiven, that can be given: walks they will take
through the old quarters, speaking of the cities

that brought them here, to Paris, to a neighborhood café
where the coffee they drink will have the fragrance

of complicity, of a friendship
that remained in its promise,

glass on glass, rain cooling
the windowpanes and the words lifting clearly

from the evening
holding them briefly in its warmth.

INSIDE THE STIR

I.

More than the meadow shaping itself under rain, than the trees
soughing their darknesses and the threads of fog

lifting from the hilltops, when we stand
inside the cool stir of air, damp with summer, and the wind

seems to answer something we want
and have no name for – the rain comes hammering

out of the beeches, and you and I and the child
are inside the cloud lying low over the valley

like somewhere we've never been,
that transforms what we think we know,

pulls the fields and quiet farms far beyond themselves
the way the rain wraps around us making us so strangely glad

inside the grey-blue rush where what we know
is how small we are, how alive

II.

All spring it has been happening, this encounter
of the irrefutables, a new child on its way,

my father ill on another continent, and each day
with its threads of happiness and worries filled

so surely with the present that time
is the unreal, the untrue −

thirty years and more I've lived like a child,
protected by love and what I chose to love,

trees and meadows and the frail bluebells
that cling to the roadbanks,
the sky with its false promise of immortality

slowly carrying its clouds across the borders,
Switzerland, Italy, those names that still spell

delight, cobblestones and belltowers and the scent
of history, where as a child I trailed enchanted

after my parents into pastry-shops and cathedrals,
and stood on the bridges
and watched the aged rivers, the Danube, the Seine,
the Arno, the Rhine;

even now those names are like a promise, even now
I want to believe there is something

to believe in, even in the promises
that cannot be kept —

years ago I had a nightmare, of workmen in a black night
digging with shovels around a pit, and my father comforted me

telling me I dreamed of death, and because he said it
it seemed death was an old acquaintance of his that knew its place

and would not bother any one of us, not then: so it was enough
to be happy inside unhappiness, or unhappy

inside happiness, it is so easy
to be unhappy, such a luxury, now at least I know

or think I know that every moment must be given
its proper weight, that when I kiss my daughter goodnight

and tuck her into her little bed
I am shaping her history, rocking her

into her hold on time the way the new child will take
its hold on time, enter the beauty

and the sadness I must be strong enough to give

III.

for Alain

There is that hour before dawn, when the birds call one by one
from their separate branches, and the sky is a dull pink over the
eastern

hills, and you are in your deep, quiet sleep, close and warm
against me; it is the hour without thoughts, of slow animal

obedience to the pull of sleep and the pull of waking, when the
child
stirs and needs to be changed, whispering to me out of her drowse;

I stand at the window with its dark light, the still lunar
greys and the meadow stiff with shadow, and I do not know

or even wonder who I am, I am simply there
inside my own stillness

that is a part of yours, that without you
would not know this gift of waking, this calm return to sleep

IV.

Deep inside there is something luminous,
something that has no end,

that must not be forgotten:
today I woke so early

and what mattered was the room bathed in gold light,
bathed in expectancy,

and I think of the mornings of white stone and lavender,
already humming with cicadas and so still with heat

that the olive tree on the far plateau seemed to shimmer
in its singleness, its bent perfection, like a symbol

of grace, of something to attain to. . .
For thirteen years the hills of the Lubéron

have guided me, not only in promise
but with the sharp, cold shadows of the cypresses in winter,

the wind from the mountains
cutting us through, making the world

transparent, vulnerable: this is what I cannot see
that then reveals itself, the clarity

I return and return to, that each time
startles me with what it contains

of truth,
cruel and forgiving −

like anything that is itself,
nothing more,

like anything I dare to resemble
or wake to

with its burden of radiance,
its gold light.

Nina Bogin was born in New York City in 1952 and has been living in France since 1976. She works as a translator specializing in art history and film subtitling. Her poems have appeared in literary magazines in the United States and abroad, including *Agenda*, *American Poetry Review*, *Ironwood*, the *Kenyon Review*, and *Stand*, and she received a National Endowment for the Arts grant in poetry in 1989. She lives in France with her husband and two daughters.

This book was designed by Tree Swenson.
The Bodoni type was set by The Typeworks, in Vancouver, B.C.
and the book was manufactured by Thomson-Shore in Ann Arbor.